Overmorrow

Janice Powell

Presentation by *BookLeaf Publishing*

Web: www.bookleafpub.com

E-mail: info@bookleafpub.com

ISBN: 9789395756969

First edition 2022

DEDICATION

For Holly,

Who said the most unforgettable words of encouragement to me regarding following my writing dreams and for her neverending wisdom on love.

ACKNOWLEDGEMENT

I would like to thank every person along the way that has encouraged me and believed in me.

PREFACE

"Whether you think you can or can't, either way you are right."

Henry Ford

"When the power of love overcomes the love of power, the world will know peace."

Jimi Hendrix

"To love oneself is the beginning of a lifelong romance."

Oscar Wilde

"A successful marriage requires falling in love many times, always with the same person."

Mignon McLaughlin

Overcomer

Wave to the waterspout from the shore
Giving it a proper farewell
Catch the waves caressing your core

Touch the tree trunks the traveling tornado tore
Taking in the tales their twisted roots tell
Wave to the waterspout from the shore

Savor the safety of the shredded sand that is sore
Soothing its stitches still itching after high tide
fell
Catch the waves caressing your core

Soak in the smoky sweet petrichor
Patiently saving its peaceful smell
Wave to the waterspout from the shore

Let the soft ripples cleanse and restore
Coaxing them to every calloused cell
Catch the waves caressing your core

Release the before to surrender for more
Leaving behind the untouched rubble of hell
Wave to the waterspout from the shore
Catch the waves caressing your core

Puddles

Watch the rain drops fall
Observe them run together
Forget the weather

Codes

Decipher your code
To know your command
It is directions for the road

If you are in lost mode
Find your soul's demand
Decipher your code

Unpack your heart's load
Examine it scaled down to grains of sand
It is directions for the road

Write to yourself an ode
To promise your purpose you will land
Decipher your code

Add to the rides you rode
To be able to count your best on one hand
It is directions for the road

Locate your node
To avoid death's door displaying your reprimand
Decipher your code
It is directions for the road

Business Casual

When will I wear today
Yesterday I wore tomorrow
It was a black tailored suit
Today I am wearing yesterday
Old clothes with holes and beat up hiking boots
Overmorrow and ereyesterday
Nothing new
But I'll start somewhere now
Even tomorrow too
Until every day is only each day
Wearing sunny business casual
Under skies bright blue
Or white silk shirts
When vacation is due
While every moment is
Me
Wearing my best shoes

Venn Diagram of Life

I slept and suffered in the west
Away from my best
Never having the money to head east
Comfort is the strongest beast
They were bubbles ready to burst
My mind lived where they overlap
In the desert sun above my cap
Pulling me like tug of war
Slowly inching their way toward being one
I pulled back in return
My skin and muscles burned
Until my arms grew weak
And I could not speak
afraid...
But patiently I became brave
Letting east reel me in
Until I could feel again
I felt like I lost
Because the journey had a cost
Until I understood
This is the way to win

Conditions

Her fire
Dim down to embers
Emerged and rose
From the wood bone and ashes
Like my eyes sent a gust of wind
Rekindling its spirit
As she froze temporarily
Needing my fuel to survive
Such beauty to watch her revive
I was air filled and seen
Dancing in the shape of her flames
No longer empty and invisible
I wanted to stay
To be a constant breeze to keep her bright
An occasional rare firenado
A column beam in the starry night
Seen from space with its raging light
It would be a breathtaking sight
But I was only a gust
And conditions out of our control
Were not right
I will never forget
Seeing me seen
Finally having a reflection
It gave me courage and might

Interdimensional Glimpse

Her eyes were a window
To another reality
For a few seconds
I saw the version of her
That loves me
Standing firmly in place while walking by

In this reality
She is blind
Or chooses to be
Too familiar with the familiar

Was she herself that day
Or another her completely

Was her first glimpse of me
Too hard to hide
Or another her completely

I know what I saw
It was fleeting but clear on her face
Like I was a camera capturing motion

Was she herself that day
Or another her completely

Did she lose her memory
Or did another dimension snatch my sanity

Bee Free

How selfish we are
As we take honey from bees
They deserve to keep

Wet Pages

Time is wet pages
When I'm with you
Too delicate to pull apart
As if they're glued
Transparent yet unreadable
Seconds blended like the words
It's fast-paced
They will dry
For our story to be told
When we die
Giving way to another version
Of Love's immortal truth

Harbor

You were a reflection of my comfort zone
Buzzing with its monotone
Did we not mold into something because of this
There is peace in repetitive sound
Like ocean waves
But at such a place we cannot be bound
We only visit to become unwound
Yet it is so tempting to stay in the town
You were a vacation
At the ocean
Not home
Your cool calm eyes like the water
Held the reflection of my comfort zone
I stood there and stared
From the shore
You were a place to help me reach for more

Fine Tune

Pain comes at low tide
On the path I only see there
I'm taking it now
But before I reach destiny
The tide changes
Washing me away in the wrong direction
With the strength of the moon
I must train my mind
To be strong like the moon
To keep waiting for low tide
Then travel faster with the fine tune

The Well

Constant war inside me
Between the militaries
Of Fire and Ice
It's a well with constant water
Where they meet
At the polar opposites
Are fires that can't be beat
Ice that will shatter on repeat
It is treacherous traveling to the well
So bad I avoid the trail
Danger lurks everywhere
I know plenty about Hell
As I live there inside my shell
Is that hope I smell
It is the only scent at the well
I need protection on the trail
Yet I don't know where to train
So my thoughts just swell
But I cannot forget how hope smells
I fight daily battles to get back to the well
Always believing one day the war will die down

Winter Moon

I'd bet my brain was a bright beam
Throughout those three ticks in time
As I saw a soul mate saunter in and out of sight
Why was I woken by such winter white
On the darkest of nights
Was it to show me what a soul mate feels like
I tell myself our eyes looked through
A two way mirror between us
That I was on the side seeing through
But I saw in her eyes she knew
The stars were aligning too
Still, she swayed away from the truth
Slipping through my fingers
Like sand made of the moon

Polaris

She will always be my north star
Her smile closest to my heart on radar
Simply from its ability to light any of my caves
Its peace I will forever save
As it holds advice constant like waves
She is my hero every day

Fate

I have this knowing
That your kiss
Would scramble me senseless
I have this longing
To reach that peak escape
I have seen the way you'd do it
With your hand resting on my face
Where no hand has ever been placed
Even though I've been kissed
I dream of your kiss,
My Darling
I have this needing
Like you're my fate

Paper Copies

Take your soul to
Sip on love by the sea
Look out as far as you can see
Take in its notes to ponder
Let them refresh you
Like cucumber water
Because love, you see,
Is as vital to the soul
As the air our bodies need to breathe

Take your soul to
Sip on love by the sea
It is nourishment to be shackle free
It gives you wings of peace

Take your soul to
Sip on love by the sea
Bring your laptop to
Take notes on what you see

Go home
Print paper copies
Of the digital copies
Let your desires be shackle free

Love will make every wish
Become your reality

One-sided

The land is magnetic
Pulling me in
It gives me a place to roam
Free
But it does not need me
For I am a breeze
It craves a vibrant creek
A natural spring
To dream on a river bed in a deep sleep

Unspoken

You spoke a different language
One only the two of us speak
One I did not know I knew
Until your eyes met mine silently
It is natural like breathing
Even when your arrival made it seem new
I must have been born with it
Carrying it dormant until you
It cannot be taught
Its words are made of heartbeats and breaths
Only our bodies command
They are urgent to be heard aloud
Steady to pass every test

The Cycle

Each of us is given a gift
So we can give the gifts
It is all a cycle
Not embracing yours
Feels lonely
Like you have been left out
Of the very universe you exist within
Be brave to shout
To give your gift
There are people that need it

Passage

I will show you love
Until you let it pass through
To vibrate from you

Forever Yours

Keep me safe with you
Infinity will fear us
For I will not part